The Sun Will Rise and So Will We

by Jennae Cecelia

The Sun Will Rise and So Will We

Cover art by Mariah Danielsen of Wander Design Co.
www.wanderdesignco.com

You are waiting for the sun to peak above
the landscape and assert its presence
in your life.
Maybe these dark days seem
long and dreary.
But what will it feel like, when your sun
rises?

The Sun Will Rise and So Will We, is a book
filled with all things sunshine without
ignoring the storms.
Pain is real. Anxiety is real.
Depression is real. Hardships in life are real.

I hope when you pick up this book you feel
heard and comforted. Even if it doesn't
seem like it right now, your sun will rise
once again, and I am cheering you on for
that moment.

You are a seed
buried deep in new soil.
Now is your time to
do the deep work
to bloom how
you want to this time.

You wake up each morning
with an unknown course
in front of you.
Questions racing through your mind.
What will today hold?
Will things ever be fine?
But please know just how important
you are to the world.
Like the sun, we need your light too.
This is a time we will look back on
and remember that we got through
these unprecedented times
because of you.

Let 2020 be the year
that opened your eyes
to see the world
a little clearer.

Tonight, the sky will paint
a message for you to remind you
that beautiful things can
come after the rain is done.
You will take it is as the sign
you have been looking for.
The glimmer in the darkness.
To go within yourself
for that light more.

I'll clean that space tomorrow.
I'll wipe it until it shines.
Oh, how I wish it was that simple
to make my mind feel fine.

It is not your responsibility
to save everyone.
Don't put that kind of
pressure on yourself.
Do the best you can
to spread your light
where you can.

Today feels heavier than most
and tomorrow might too.
There is uncertainty
lingering in the air.
But I have hope.
I have strength.
Those are two things
I can control.
I will get past
all of this unknown.

I am learning through this all
how to stand tall,
but forgiving myself when
I shrink a little from
the heavy weight on my shoulders.
It is okay to acknowledge that things are
hard to hold sometimes,
while also recognizing I have the
strength in me to keep going.

I am growing.
I have so much to gain.
From the hill tops with sunrises
and the fields with sunsets.
I am watching as I grow
and the earth does too.
We are all growing right now,
even if it is into something unexpected.
It is the growth that helps us bloom.

It is as if I want my worst fears
to come true so I can say,
 "See I told you that would happen.
I told you that could happen."
It is something I want
so badly to be wrong about,
but also want to be right about
to prove that I wasn't wrong in
thinking that way.

I want to be the
golden hour girl.
Beams of happiness
coming from me.
Not a cloud in sight.
My storm is hidden
by my constant
need to be the light.

Dear Present Me,

There are sunrises over here.
Coffee you will savor and
not chug to stay awake.
You smile more than not.
When the rain does fall
you allow it to hit your cheeks
and know that is good for you.
You found light over here
in the midnight moon.
I can't wait for you to see.

Love,
Future Me

It is hard to do things
on your own.
Hold walls up,
maintain the roof,
and put a smile on
even when times are
tough to get through.
Don't forget that
you are made for than
holding up everyone else.
Make sure you are
loving yourself.

While you are picking up
everyone else's pieces,
don't forget you have
pieces to pick up
for yourself too.
You can't pour from
a broken glass.
Take time for you.

This season may not have bloomed
the way you wanted.
Maybe you are a seed still in the ground.
Accept your growth where it is at
and surrender your need to force
what will come when it is ready.

Sometimes you have to
love people from a distance.
You have the right to
create boundaries.
You have the right to
not pick up the phone
and listen.

I am the journal with coffee stains
and flowers tucked between the pages.
I am the journal filled with words
you will never hear
come out of my mouth
and sentences that are either
scribbled or perfectly legible.
I am the journal that embraces it all.

You can live for your
next vacation,
when the bell rings,
the after-work drinks,
the warmer days,
the sunnier mornings,
the Friday nights that lead
into Saturday mornings.
You can live in a constant waiting
for what you perceive as
better times.
But how many little moments
are you missing
that truly make up your life?

I am afraid that I will
let people down.
I am the trunk supporting
everyone's branches
and I don't know how to
stay standing.

My life may be full
of uncertain weather,
but the skies always clear
and things come back
even better.

I may not rise from my soil
at the same time
everyone else is in bloom.
But they needed their time to shine,
I am waiting for more room.

You are a star pushed far away
from all of the rest.
Maybe it is time for you
to shine on yourself for a while.
Recognize that you can still
see all the other stars,
even if for now it is from a distance.

Maybe I landed on
the dark side of the moon.
The side I thought
I would never see.
But what if all I have to do is
keep moving forward,
slowly or fast,
to get back to
where I want to be?
Even if it has new scenery.

The goodbyes weren't said.
The *I'll miss you* hugs weren't given.
Because things stopped
without my permission.
So here I am,
saying it in a whisper from afar,
but it is screaming in my head.
I love you.
I'll miss you.
This isn't goodbye though.
It is a new beginning.
Not an end.

These roads are unknown.
The scenery is different.
No familiar face in sight.
The lack of normality
makes it hard
to breathe on my own.
But every place becomes the norm
the longer you stick around.
Take a deep breath.
You won't always be new
to this unknown town.

These times will go by
in the blink of an eye.
A whisper in the wind.
Then they will be the moments
you look back on with nostalgia.
As you sip your coffee
and remember how it tasted
back then when you were
up until 4 AM.
Right now, it feels
hard and never ending,
but one day it will be
pieces in your memory
that you struggle
to put back together.
Enjoy today.
For you have so many tomorrows.

Where do you feel the most alone?
At home between you
and your four walls?
In the streets as people pass,
but don't make eye contact?
We aren't really alone,
we just get lost in the loudness of life
and forget that to see and be seen,
we need to take it slow and quiet.

Today I ask for strength
to hold myself
and the people I love up.
To be the glue for them,
but also, myself.
No foundation will hold
unless I pour into me too.

The past is behind you.
If you want new beginnings,
then stop looking back.
Stop reliving the past.
Shift your focus
to the future you can have.

We have parted ways unexpectedly.
Grieving from afar of all the things
we didn't know could be taken away.
Memories lost.
Photos that won't be captured.
Moments in time we can't replace.
But just remember
for every memory lost,
there are always new ones to make.

I am finding myself longing
for the moments that
I once looked at as small.
The hum of coffee shop chatter
and glasses clinking in celebration.
Now I am realizing
it is those moments
that mean most of all.

meet me for coffee

You are there for me,
whether sunrays or raindrops
linger on my face.
Into your arms as I rise or fall.
You are my safe place.

One day came
and one day went.
So when are you going
to make it happen?
Are you really going to say,
one day again?

I bloomed my own flowers
faster than waiting
for someone to purchase me some.

There is nothing wrong
with the seeds you are planting.
You are just in an environment
that doesn't encourage growth.
It is time to move somewhere
you can fully bloom as yourself.

It isn't that their life
is better than yours,
you just see them when
their lights are turned on
and windows wide open.
Everyone has problems
behind closed curtains.

Waiting is a game
I don't want to be a player in.
I'll sit out this round.
But it is in the waiting
that I learned
to have faith
what I need will be found.

Jennae Cecelia

I want to tell you this today,
as you wish for things to go back
to how they were before.
Hold on to the todays you have
just a little bit more.
Even with all the uncertainty,
don't forget these days
are still worth living for.

Even here in the unknown,
beautiful things can grow.

I will flourish in my new soil.
I will miss the old,
but all I can do is go from
where I have been planted.
I have no choice but to grow.

Here I bloom because I want to.
Not because I was told
to smile and look pretty.
I bloom for myself now.
I always knew I had it within me.

You may feel like you have
a blind date with
next month,
next week,
or even later today.
The excitement mixed
with nervousness
both come into play.
Just know that even though
uncertainty is present,
there will be a time when you can say
that you know where you are going
beyond just this moment.

You didn't climb all this way,
to ignore the view
and just keep walking
to the next place
that is a goal for you.

I want to remember these days.
The ones where we
ate a whole watermelon on the front patio
while sipping a mango sour beer.
The days we drove around the city
that is always booming without traffic
with iced coffees dripping in condensation.
When life was simple again.
When the world woke and saw that
connection was all they wanted.

I watched as the fear
washed down the drain
in a circular motion
until I could no longer
see the pain.
I washed my hands
of what was hurting me most.
But now how do I go about
not getting my hands
full of fear again?

The snow will fall over
the old footprints
and everything will look
perfectly put together.
But we don't know
what is truly buried beneath.
We don't really know
what the aftermath is
when people face
their unwanted weather.

I can still bloom after so long,
of wilted leaves and lack of sun.
I can still rise even after a fall.

I am a crack in the sidewalk
that keeps being filled with hope
that I won't break again.
Why doesn't anyone ask if
there is more they can do
than just patch up my flaws
and hope they won't have to
see or hear about them again?

"Don't forget to be thankful
for another day
where you wake up
with the sun,"
they say.
But it is okay not to be okay.
Lay low and take it slow.
Having a bad day
doesn't make you ungrateful.

I took a wrong turn.
Hit a dead end.
Wrong turn again.
But I am on my way.
That's what matters.
At least I am still driving
with my destination in mind.
I could have just given up
on the roadside.

Your star brought me
more light,
but I am the moon
so even without you
I can see just fine.

I was looking for
an unexpected gleam
of yellow and orange
amongst the stormy
clouds above.
Are you there?
I'll keep waiting here.
Praying here.
That you will come
back to me.

Anxiety has a way of robbing me
from living in the present.
I worry about what the future holds.
Children?
Illnesses?
Debt?
I dwell on things
I did in the past.
Waving hi to the wrong person.
Saying, "you too" to the waitress who
definitely wasn't about to
enjoy her meal.
Anxiety has a way
of making me feel
like I am moving forwards
and backwards
but neither one
lasts.

The horizon is a good place to look at,
but don't forget about the ground
you are walking on right now.

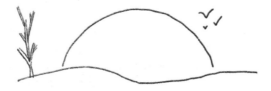

This season may not be
full of growth for you,
but maybe it should be
full of reflection.
So that in time you are
ready to bloom
in the right direction.

Never stop asking
those big questions
or moving with
an adventurous heart.
You have so much good to come.
This is just the start.

You have the power to live out
your own story.
Don't change the script
to please someone else.
You read beautifully
by yourself.

You can't stay in today forever.
Whether it is good or bad.
Whether you want to or not.
Nothing is permanent.
It is beautiful and tragic
all at once.

You may feel like you are constantly
back and forth between
the messy chaos
and the calm.
But that is where you discover
the most about yourself.

Even in the unknown,
kindness can grow.
Kindness needs no certainty,
just hope.

I know you are afraid
to take that next step.
But you have to
move either way,
so make it towards
the direction you
want to get.

Life doesn't come with a blueprint
for you to place on a wall
and look at for guidance.
Life is about drawing free-hand as you go
and not anticipating things to be provided.

My legs haven't seen the sun
in at least five years.
My legs haven't jumped into a pool
or a lake since I discovered
that I am supposed to critique my body
and fill it with words of hate.
But now as I enter into later years of life,
I realized my legs have missed out on a lot
and all because someone once somewhere
that means nothing to me now,
laughed as I sat out on a dock.

I want to feel fearless.
Moving easy with the wind.
Fine with any direction I go.
I want to be an adventurous soul,
but I find safety at home.

The night comes quick with darkness
that I am not ready to face.
So I wake up with the sun,
to spend as much time with her
in my safe place.

The clouds are lingering
around the space
the light should be
pouring through.
Whispers from the wind that it
will come back soon.

Their season may appear
to have more pleasurable weather
than yours.
Sunshine looks ever present,
while you have lingering clouds.
But just know we all
weather differently.
We never know what it
truly feels like
until we experience
their weather ourselves.

I will no longer call myself a mess.
Yes, I have papers scattered.
There is a coffee mug tower in the sink.
The mail looks like
I have been out of town for weeks.
But this is the first time I am happy,
even if my house may not look like it.
Just because my house is put together
does not mean I feel put together
inside this body I call home.

Don't forget the roads
you have crossed.
The accomplishments
checked off your bucket list.
Maybe right now
you feel in a stand still,
but don't forget
all of your progress.

Although today may feel
heavy to hold.
Just know tomorrow
will bring light.
You won't always be
carrying such a heavy load.

All the places you want to go
are waiting for you
with welcome signs.
You just have to drive.
You just have to stop saying
this isn't the right time.

Match your breath to the breeze.
Don't forget all you need.
Simply sit in the silence around you.
Take in today.
Let go of tomorrow.
Worry about it when it comes.

Your strengths may seem
like they are off in the distance
far from reach,
but once you accept
the love you deserve
you will realize they are
closer than you think.

Going where it is comfortable
and accepting what is happening?
No.
Going with the flow
is no longer acceptable.

Today is the best day
to dive deep within yourself.
Jump in arms wide open.
Ready to embrace
what comes with the fall.
Dive deep within yourself
and discover
all that is hidden.
There is more to this all.

Hope is on the horizon.
Hope is the yellow brightness peeking out,
not quite on full display.
Hope will wait for you.
Hope doesn't go away.

Today could be the day
you look back at in
five,
ten,
twenty years
and say,
"The decision I made
that day is what got me
here today."

I don't know what is to come
past the horizon I am on today.
But I am moving forward
on these trails with hope that things
will go the right way.

Today is here to tell you
that it is proud you made it this far.
With all the setbacks in life,
it is glad you chose to press forward
even when it was hard.

They might not understand
the path you chose,
but remind them that those steps
are yours to take.
The ones with setbacks
and growth.
They are yours to make.

The streets are empty
and it is hard
not to feel the same way.
Too much room
for my thoughts to wander.
Will I be ok?
But the streets will fill again,
and my mind will become busy too.
This is a moment in time
that will be hard,
but I will make it through.

The sun rose
and the neon *open* signs turned on.
Hold onto that hope.
We will see dawn.

I miss wrapping my arms
around you.
You feel so far away
yet so close.
Like a mirage
out in the distance.
I swear you are here.
I swear I can see you.
I swear I feel your presence.
Send me a sign.
A feather in the wind.
You are here.
I can feel it.

My mind makes me feel
like loneliness only lives in me.
That everyone else is free.
But in reality,
we are all a little alone.
We just feel like
we are the only ones
that have loneliness invade our homes.

You still have time to do
what you dream up for your life.
It is never too late
to chase your dreams
like catching butterflies.

I like it here.
Where the unknown meets certainty.
Slowly walking the line between,
like it is a fallen tree branch.
I like it where I know enough,
but not too much.
There is no excitement in a
perfectly paved path.

I am strong but I am soft too.
I can hold my own,
but oh, how I melt into you.
Not because I have to.
I want to.

Waiting.
We are waiting.
For answers.
For the, *good to go*.
For the green light.
For this weight to be lifted.
We are all waiting.
I hope you find comfort in knowing
that you aren't alone in the waiting.

The earth is shaking
and you don't know how you are going
to hold up for much longer.
But your walls are stronger than you think.
You are stronger than you think.
You might have to take it
easy for a while,
but this won't crush you.
You have faced this feeling before
and come out with more.

You are realizing that
what matters most
doesn't come wrapped in bows.
Conversation and community
are what you would rather be gifted.
Reconnecting relationships
that have drifted.

You ask for time to slow down,
so you can truly
soak in the moment.
To breath in today.
To move slower through life.
Sip your tea and notice the flavors.
Really feel the grass between your toes.
Find the shapes in the clouds again.
Here is your time.
Don't let it go by unnoticed.

I am messy.
Like unmade bed sheets
in the morning.
Red wine spilt on the white carpet
at your mother's house.
Hair thrown in a bun.
But oh how I create in the mess.
Messy spaces lead to
beautiful creations.

We are learning through this all
that every person holds value
no matter how small.
You never know who you
will rely on the most.
Let go of your ego.

This is alone time.
To sit with just yourself
and the day.
Laughing and talking
to yourself only.
That is okay.
It is not weird to be alone.
It is not scary to be alone.
Unless you are afraid of finding out
more about yourself.
But maybe you *need* to find out
more about yourself.

Maybe you want to fit in.
Lost amongst the crowd.
Not standing out.
Blending in.
Camouflaged,
but not totally hidden.
Why are you so afraid to be seen?
You never know who in this world
might take your story,
or your smile,
or your advice
and feel seen too.
Everyone has something
someone else needs.

They aren't the author of your book,
the painter of your canvas,
or the speaker at your talk.
So why are you letting other people
choose if you do those things or not?

Let me ask you this as you say
you want a better life,
a new life,
a happier life-
are you ready for things
to get harder
before they get better?
Are you willing to dive deep
within yourself
and change your negative thoughts
about yourself and the world?
You can't flood yourself
with negativity
and question why
nothing positive
is flowing to you.

For once I don't feel alone
even though I am physically alone.
Which is hard to wrap my mind around.
For once it feels like the whole world
is experiencing the anxiousness
I have held for so long and
many never understood.
It hurts me that people are
feeling that pain too,
but oh is it comforting to know
I am not so alone
in those feelings anymore.

I feel like I am on
a balance beam between
take care of others,
but also myself.
Don't be selfish,
but don't over give
and deplete myself.
I feel like I am constantly wondering
if I did enough for my friends,
my family,
my coworkers,
and still myself.
Self-care.
Self-love.
It isn't selfish.
But sometimes I just feel like
giving more to others than myself,
and I think that is more than alright.
Learn what that balance looks like
for you and your life.

Right now you may feel like
you have been forced out of
your comfort zone.
Maybe that is a good thing.
Have you been craving growth?
Have you been wanting
to reach new marks in life?
No big changes happen when
you are comfortable.
Maybe this is the Universe's way
of telling you this is your time.

Nothing is promised but this moment.
Do we ever truly meet the future?

You are pulling weeds out
of your garden.
Over
and over
and over
and over.
But isn't it worth it to uncover
all of the growth you didn't see
because you let your life pile up
with unwanted weeds?

The next step doesn't have to
get you to the finish line right away.
It doesn't even have to
get you to the path.
You just have to turn your attention to
the direction you want to get.

Let the morning sun
peeking through the blinds
be a sign that light
is ready to shine in your life.

Today has fresh air
you have never smelt
and sunrays
you have never felt.
Today is a chance to restart.

The sun will rise again
and so will we.
Things will get greener.
Things will get warmer.
Everything will grow again
and so will we.

To read more work by Jennae Cecelia, check out her other seven books:

Bright Minds Empty Souls

Uncaged Wallflower

I Am More Than a Daydream

Uncaged Wallflower Extended Edition

I Am More Than My Nightmares

Dear Me At Fifteen

Losing Myself Brought Me Here

https://www.amazon.com/Jennae-Cecelia/e/B01M6UEGVY?ref=sr_ntt_srch_l nk_1&qid=1587131963&sr=8-1

About the author

www.jennaececelia.com

@JennaeCecelia on Instagram

Jennae Cecelia is a best-selling author of inspirational poetry books
and is best known for her book, Uncaged Wallflower.

She is also in inspirational speaker who digs into topics like
self-love, self-care, mental health, and body positivity.

Her mission is to encourage people to reach their
full potential and live a life filled with positivity and love.

Jennae Cecelia